Dandelion

An Ozark Mountain Reflection

Susan Steele Rives

Quill & Stylus Press

Copyright © 2024. Susan Steele Rives.

Photo Credit: Abigail Taylor
Stephen Rives, Illustrator

All rights reserved. No part of this book may be reproduced in any form or by any electronic or mechanical means, including information storage and retrieval systems, without permission in writing from the publisher, except by reviewers who may quote brief passages in a review.

Published by Quill & Stylus Press, Springfield, MO.
Printed in the United States of America.

ISBN 979-8-9903586-0-7 Hardcover
ISBN 979-8-9903586-1-4 Softcover
ISBN 979-8-9903586-2-1 E-book
ISBN 979-8-9903586-3-8 Audiobook

Battlefield published previously at www.sapphirevisions.com.

The Pen references a quote by Edward Bulwer-Lytton from *Richelieu; Or, The Conspiracy*, 1839, though similar iterations of the sentiment had been written much earlier.

Contents

1. Dedication — 1
2. Introduction — 4
3. Blank Page — 6
4. This House Is Too Quiet! — 8
5. The Words in My Head — 9
6. Photograph — 10
7. The Thief — 11
8. The Pen — 12
9. The Greatest Weapon — 13
10. Dissonance — 14
11. The Untimely Demise of My Dear Uncle Sam — 17
12. Silence — 21
13. Battleground — 22
14. Mama, Let Me Come — 24
15. Autumn Air — 26
16. As she weeps — 28
17. The Widow's Might — 29

18.	All Things New	30
19.	The Minister and His Message	32
20.	Chicken Soup	34
21.	The Path	37
22.	Evening Slumber	38
23.	Spirit Wind	40
24.	More of You	41
25.	Fair Thee as a Feather	42
26.	Victor Won	43
27.	Buried Treasure	44
28.	Rhythmic Lullaby	45
29.	Water from the Well	47
30.	The Riddled Door	48
31.	A Riddle for My Son	50
32.	Dandelion	53
33.	My Dream	54
34.	Word Waltz	58
35.	Soft Falls the Rain	59
36.	The Grand, Majestic Ball	60
37.	Take Me Somewhere	62
38.	Still	67
39.	Grieve No More	68
40.	A Slave to Christ	72

41. Old Man's Clothes	74
42. The Potter	76
43. Empty-handed	78
44. Carry On	80
45. Where Did the Time Go?	82
46. Let the Children Come!	84
47. King of My Heart	86
48. Clean Hands and A Pure Heart	87
49. About the Author	89

Dedicated with love to my family and friends.

For
Ben, Abigail, Flora, Rosie, and Arthur
John and Sarah
Noah and Julia
&
Grace

May this book bring peace and hope to you. I pray that your hope lies in Christ alone, for He is the only one worthy of it. May He be your treasure forever.

SPECIAL THANKS

To Ruth, Mel, and Jennie: Thank you for your encouragement and for letting me bounce around ideas with you – even the silly ones.

To Dana and Randy: Thank you for listening to me, dreaming with me, and giving of yourselves when we needed it most.

To my dearest friends and my brothers and sisters in Christ: Thank you for your love and friendship and for pointing me ever toward the Cross. Words are just not enough to express my gratitude.

To the Knights. I will always believe that we have the best team anywhere! Each of you holds a very special and permanent place in my heart. Thank you, Kristin. Your friendship means the world to me.

To Tayla: Thank you so much for your encouragement and feedback. I am eager to see more of your writing soon!

To the precious infant whose tiny footprints I borrowed: I pray that the One who knit you together in your mother's womb would cause your feet to chase after Him all the days of your life.

To Nicholas S.: Your courage and resolve at a pivotal moment in time did not escape my notice, and it prompted one of the poems that follows. I pray you will continue to exemplify what it means to stand up and boldly proclaim what is right and true.

To Shelley and Stacey: Friends are friends forever. No matter how far apart we are, we always seem to be able to pick up right where we left off. I am quite certain I could not have come this far without you. I especially appreciate the encouragement you have given to me in regard to my writing in general and this book specifically. Thank you. I love you both.

I am thankful to the Lord for each of you. I am thankful to the Lord for who He is and what He has accomplished for His glory. May His name be praised, and may He be our hope and joy forever!

Introduction

Welcome to the world of the dandelion. Imagine growing up between the cracks in a sidewalk where nothing else can survive. Picture the landscaper who makes it his job to rid pristine lawns of the pesky little weed. Now envision a wild Ozark country meadow teeming with bright yellow blossoms or a toddler blowing wishes into the wind.

The journey we are about to embark on is much like the one I just described. It begins with sorrow, desperation, conflict, and pain. Even those among us who are not dandelions have experienced the torment of tragedy or the sharp sting of suffering, trauma, or heartache. Yet because we are on a journey, we will not stay in our present or past grief. We must move forward from darkness to light—and hope.

Along this pathway, you will encounter poems such as confessions, historical narratives, ballads, and riddles. Many of these are written from the perspective of the poet, though certain pieces are crafted empathetically, written through the eyes of others, some of whom I have known personally.

You may come across some lines or stanzas in the poems that seem out of place or perhaps discombobulated. My dad would have called them *cattywampus*. I will leave it to you to discover where these cattywampus verses are and what their purpose is. They *do* have a purpose. Sometimes chicken soup is just chicken soup, and sometimes it is not soup at all!

Finally, you will find a collection of song lyrics. I pray that the words within these pages will be cause for hope, joy, contemplation, and reflection. All glory to Christ!

This page was intentionally left blank, though no one is quite sure why –

perhaps to make you question it; perhaps to make you sigh.

This House Is Too Quiet!

This house is too quiet! Now, where are the mice
who sift through the flour and pilfer the rice?

And where are the tomcats who chase them around,
hide and go seek, here a leap, there a bound?

And where still the dog, so annoyed by the cats?
He must be out on the porch taking a nap.

And what of the boy whose dog tolerates cats?
Or the girl whose cats long for the mice they can't catch?

They too are gone, and their mama's heart sighs,
"This house is too quiet! Now, where are the mice?"

The Words in My Head

The many words inside my head
    Are meant to sleep when I'm in bed.
Rather, they churn and yearn and burn,
And make me twist and toss and turn.
Then when their order they have learned,
    Emerge as poetry instead.

I neatly place them in their rows,
    Counting meter as I go.
The words, they clamor, screech, and shout,
Bellow loudly, softly pout.
Then when, at last, they stand up stout,
    My blessing on them I bestow.

For they are subject to my whim,
    These words that in my head do swim.
I do my very best to tame
Unruly words that play their game.
One day, perhaps, I'll earn my claim
    As a master of rhyme and synonym.

Photograph

Life through a lens appears merry and bright –
  smiling faces and joyful delight.
  Pleasantly staged to grant memories for years:
  family, friends, and abounding good cheer.
  But lenses can't capture the same as can words,
  the thoughts and emotions not seen and not heard.
  Tucked away under the glossy veneer
  may be loneliness, heartache, dishonesty, fear.
  Impressions forever portrayed upon film
  may be real or they might be a farce -
  Either sharing the sweet charm of family and friends,
  or hiding indelible scars.

The Thief

A cruel deceiver, surely it is.
  It's here, and then it's gone.
  Looking off into distant horizon,
  Then suddenly, upon you it's come.

  He says that he gave ample warning.
  For my part, I'm not sure.
  Crept upon me as a thief
  Who in the shadows lurked.

  Now, alas, he's come and gone, and
  Never shall return.
  Keep your babies close, my love,
  Before the hour turns.

The Pen

"The pen is mightier than the sword,"
   I heard a wise man say.
   By it have many millions met their death.
From blood-red ink on fashioned nib
The vain decrees go out
   As kings exact from men their dying breath.

Woe to kings and *noble* men
Who wield their pens as sword,
Who snuff out life with single downward stroke.
Dismissive, without mercy,
   Laying waste to what is good,
   They blot out souls, for they have none of their own.

And woe to them who think
Their wicked deeds will go unseen.
They'll only be obscured but for a while.
Then there will come a reckoning -
Of this you can be sure -
Exposing their duplicitous revile.

The Greatest Weapon

The greatest weapon known to man
Does not bear sharpened blade.
Does not hold shells or bullets.
Is not by smithy made.

By it nations rise to power.
By it nations fall.
By it wisdom marches on
Or comes to grinding halt.

For though the weapon is not sword,
Two edges still it has.
In strength arising to defend,
In weakness to attack.

Dissonance

One hundred cannons. Blasting guns.
    Screeching whistles. Pounding drums.
    Roaring lions on the prowl.
    Charlatans selling their wares.

    Raging fires. Smoky haze.
    Rising flood waters. Chaotic days.
    Unbridled lying. Wicked truth.
    Unspeakable cold reality.

    Bolt the door. Silence the waves.
    Put on your blinders. Flee to be saved.
    Quiet your spirit. Nourish your soul
    While the turmoil rampages and fury spews.

The lawlessness never ceases to be
And the dissonance reaches toward eternity.
We cannot ignore but we must not be ruled
By the violent tempest, tumultuous, cruel.

While shackled humanity makes its noise
Seeking to devastate and destroy,
Pilfering, pillaging peace and joy
We patiently long for that day.

My friend, do not be held captive to
The ones who would seek your demise and ruin.
Clear out the cobwebs. Renew your mind
That peace and light your soul may find.

The Untimely Demise of My Dear Uncle Sam

I received the somber news
   as sun set low today.
My beloved Uncle Sam
   by death was swept away.

It wasn't on the battlefield that
   he met his demise.
'Twas long before when men ignored
   the counsel of the wise.

Through hazy blue and smoky gray
   the soldiers made their case.
With bayonets each man fought for
   the cause his heart embraced.

Surely some were justified
in what they thought was right.
Others fell as Justice found
their motives dark as night.

Languish we in mourning
as the distant fiddles play,
for my beloved Uncle Sam
has left and gone away.

Foreboding fears meet
bitter tears
As distant fiddles play,
For my beloved Uncle Sam
Has left and gone away.

Silence

Silence is what I must find today.
　There is no other means that I know
　To quiet the incessant chatter I hear
　That causes me only to doubt and to fear.
　I must find a quiet place so to draw near
　To the voice of the One who makes all things clear.

'Tis not an audible voice that I seek
In the thunder, the wind, or the rain,
But rather, His words written so long ago
That are worth more to me than fine silver or gold –
Words that speak life to my trembling soul.
Words that will silence the greatest of foes.

For on the great precipice now do I stand.
I do not wish to fall or to fail.
Lord, please rescue me from this world's evil snare
And the glittery trinkets of Vanity Fair.
Oh, Lord, that You would be my only care,
I humbly offer You this, my prayer.

Battleground

A young man steps upon a stage of frozen crumpled grass
   Unwitting volley, smiling grand debut.
   His colleagues take their places, and, as all in one accord,
   They smile also, coming in on cue.

   Their glee expressions stand against
   the stone-cold hearts of men,
   Their cheering met with glaring evil deed.
   For amidst their peaceful proclamation of the good,
   Their words are pummeled soundly by a beat.

   One by one, the thunder seeks to slay them
   where they stand and
   Drop them to the cold and frozen ground, and
   Yet the voice of good remains from sea to shining sea
   Mustering courage, in our hearts it pounds.

   The good, it cries out for the one
   whose voice was never heard,
   Millions who have met an early grave
   Silenced by the pens of men who placed themselves above
   The innocents that they were sworn to save.

How vile, how wicked, have men come to be?
Their own they would willingly slay.
And those who uphold and defend sacred life
Are mocked and are held in disdain?

Yet brightly a candle-light still remains.
The Good, it still prevails.
And men who would come against innocent life –
The born, the unborn, and young men alike –
Will face their Maker one last time,
For the Good, it still prevails.

Young men of courage take heart and take heed,
To the grand stage of life you ascend.
Let your words be of comfort, for hope, and for good, and
May the kingdom of Light know no end.

Mama, Let Me Come

Oh, Mama, won't you let me come and
   stay with you a while?
   I promise not to cry too much.
   I'll even make you smile.

Sometimes I hear you weeping, and
   I know that you're afraid.
   I'm not sure I was on the list of
   all the plans you'd made.

But that's okay, Mom. I've heard that
   surprises can be fun!
   And if you let me come and play,
   I'll show you more than one!

I'll show you how I startle, and
   you'll hear me when I coo.
   The next surprise you'll notice is that
   I look just like you!

Before you even blink an eye
   you'll hear me try to talk.
   Then one day I'll be big enough to
   hold your hand and walk.

Could you please read me stories, Mom?
I'll listen even now.
Did you know I can hear your voice
each time you speak out loud?

Yes, I can feel your touches
when you rub your stomach so.
Can you feel me when I kick?
Can you see how fast I grow?

Oh, Mama, aren't you happy that
you'll get to see me soon?
I can hardly wait until
I get to see you, too!

Oh, Mama, please, please let me
come and play with you a while.
Don't cause my tender life to end
before I see your smile.

You're so beautiful Mama.
I love you already.

Autumn Air

I felt the brisk, cool autumn air and
  Saw the harvest moon's soft stare.
  My heart became alive, aware;
  Began to love, began to care.

'Twas not infatuation but
  The deepest, truest, purest love –
  Built on hope and forged in trust,
  Made of forever-thoughts, it was.

Alas, forever could not be.
  True love mocked by reality.
  Day turned to night, and land to sea,
  Alone, adrift in agony.

For once that fire so brightly burned
  As if the world would ever turn.
  One soul wandered; one soul yearned.
  Unrequited love now spurned.

A-sea, alone, tossed to and fro
Uncertain which way I would go.
Relying on the Wind to blow and
Gently, safely see me home.

Then one night I gazed up and saw
The brilliance of ten billion stars
Illuminating my path home, and
Showing me where I belong.

Marvelous Light! I followed thus.
Joy restored. A deeper trust.
Beauty from ashes, adrift no more.
Rising sun on golden shore.

Standing now upon dry ground
New strength and courage I have found.
My heart unencumbered to love and to share
As I breathe in so deeply the crisp autumn air.

As she weeps

My food no longer tastes sweet, my love.
    There's no savor upon my tongue.
    I never knew how much my life
    Upon your shoulders hung.

    Wine that once brought happiness
    And filled us with good cheer
    Now tastes bitter to my lips
    When mixed with mournful tears.

    Oh, how the songs you would sing to me
    Brought laughter and a smile!
    These are distant memories
    As I walk this lonely mile.

    You would urge me to carry on,
    And carry on I will
    Until the sun sets one last time
    Over yonder hill.

The Widow's Might

Oh, Lord, I cannot carry on without my dearest love.
   You know how very much he meant to me.
   And yet you placed me here right now.
   For what I do not know.
   Please help me understand and let me see.

My lips confess that you, O Lord,
Are worth more than fine gold,
My treasure both for now and evermore.
I pray you give me strength from day to day to persevere
Though I am frail and weak and tired and poor.

Yet when I'm at my lowest Lord, my eyes gaze up at you,
And I remember then your promise true,
That you will never leave me,
Nor will you forsake me Lord.
Your Spirit stays with me, my soul renews.

O Lord, you are my strength
when I'm too weak to weather on.
I have not strength my own on which to draw.
Please help me keep my eyes on you,
not to the left or right,
And hear my pleas when on your name I call.

All Things New

He cannot hurt you now, my love,
   Can't hurt you anymore.
He cannot reach beyond the chasm
Nor step foot through yonder door.

Blood was spilt and wounds inflicted.
Bruises I can see on you.
In your eyes, your countenance,
I see the pain he put you through.

Come, sit with me. Come, sit, and rest.
I'll dry your anguished tears.
I'll hold you tight within my arms,
And calm your deepest fears.

I will not leave your side, my love.
Your soul, it longs for peace.
I will not leave you all alone
In sorrow, torment, grief.

And one day, love, when least you think,
Your darkness will give way
To light and hope and all things good.
You'll see a brand new day!

This pain, though it is heavy, dear,
Will all be over soon.
A brand new dawn is coming when
All things will be made new.

The Minister and His Message

He sits behind his humble desk and
   studies there for hours,
   Parsing Greek and Hebrew
   verbs and nouns,
   Exegeting scripture verse by verse and
   line by line,
   Praying for God's wisdom and His power.

He knows that he's mere mouthpiece for the
words that must be said, and
Prays again that God would guide him
through the text he's read.
For there the good news of Christ Jesus
shows on every page, and
Redemptive history unfolds
displaying God's great grace.

For in God's perfect garden,
Adam sinned against his Lord, and
All mankind was sentenced
thus to death.
Centuries of sacrifice,
the blood of bulls and goats
Could not atone or satisfy God's wrath.

But then the spotless Lamb of God,
our Lord incarnate came
To ransom His creation
from their plight.
For only He, the sinless Man,
our God in flesh, could free
His chosen from their sinful,
darkest night.

And save He did by His own blood!
He conquered sin and death!
He took our heart of stone,
gave us a brand new heart of flesh!
He took our dry bones, gave them life,
gave us His very breath.
And now, in love, He bids us come
to follow Him in faith.

And so the pastor studies,
line by line and word by word
That Christ may be exalted and
His message may be heard.
He prays for, teaches, nurtures
all the sheep under his care.
He boldly speaks the truth in love;
Christ's message must be shared.

Yes, he calls them to repentance that in turn,
they will believe, and
Those who heed the call of Christ
their Savior will receive.

Chicken Soup

Today my friends and family
   came in from out of town.
I made my secret recipe,
   enough to go around.

A pot of steaming soup it was.
I cooked a double batch,
Put together lovingly,
   entirely from scratch.

I started with fresh chicken, onions,
celery, and broth.
I added in some carrots,
boiled all 'til it was hot.

And then the special blend I used
that's secret to this day
Was added to the soup I served
to all my guests today.

Some of them weren't hungry,
others too engrossed to care.
A couple were delighted that
I'd cooked enough to share.

Those who ate agreed –
it was the best soup they had tried.
Some said not a single word and
seemed preoccupied.

I'll be eating soup, I'm sure,
for several days to come.
I'll love and savor every bite.
Stop by – I'll serve you some!

It's clear that this soup isn't
everybody's cup of tea, so
I'll enjoy it – yes I will!!
There's plenty left to eat.

The Path

In a chorus of Queen Anne's Lace,
Purple clover all around,
Hides a narrow meandering path
Not so easily found.

It walks by the whispering wood,
treads lightly near jagged peaks.
It skips by the cool spring waters,
Runs free near the merry creek.

It pauses by a tall, wise oak tree
and greets the warm rising sun.
It lingers in the meadow,
Then once again it runs!

Back by the wise old oak tree,
Splashing through the playful creek,
Skipping by the fishing pond, but
Softly near the peaks.

Home once again to Queen Anne's Lace,
Purple clover all around,
Lies a tired but joyful meandering path
Not so easily found.

Evening Slumber

Purple mountain in the distance,
Golden crown upon its head.
Blue green ribbons dance aloft
Until, at last, they go to bed.

Nestled 'neath a starry blanket
Gentle slumber for the night.
Resting in God's grace and peace,
Awaiting morning glory's light.

Spirit Wind

Wind, O Wind,
   From where art thou
   That bloweth over branch and bough
   Or, silent, gently toucheth leaves,
   Or restless, ravages the seas?
   Come thou from the deepest night
   Where man hath neither breath nor sight?
   Or come thou from the lofty heights
   Where hopes do soar and wings take flight?
   I cannot see you, but I hear –
   Your voice calls out so loud and clear
   on one day. Yet, the very next,
   Your stillness leaves me quite perplexed.
   Wind, O Wind,
   Please blow away
   The clouds that, stubborn, still remain
   That I might finally, clearly see
   The destiny thou hast for me.

More of You

If one thing this New Year may see,
Please let it be more Christ in me.

I do not wish for wealth or fame,
But rather, glory for His name.

May I decrease, and He abound,
My hope in Him alone be found.

His blood which was for sinners spilt
Doth now remove my shame and guilt.

His righteousness, now counted mine,
That through me His own light could shine.

One prayer I have, Lord, may it be –
More of you and less of me.

Fair Thee as a Feather

Fair thee as a mother
    as she waits for newborn cry.
    Fair thee as a father
    as he trains his son to fly.

    Fair thee as a falcon
    rising ever toward the sun.
    Fair thee as a runner
    when his race is nearly done.

    Fair thee as a feather
    floating gently on the breeze.
    Fair thee as a mariner
    at rest on placid seas.

Victor Won

War is over. Victor Won.
   Weapons laid down. Battle done.

Rebels banished per behest of
Victor-King's triumphant quest.

Some, though rebels once, have now
Surrendered to the Kingdom's Crown.

Though enemies, He made them friends,
Brought animosity to end.

For though they once against Him fought,
With His own blood, their souls He bought.

Grateful former foes now sing
In praise of their new Victor-King.

Buried Treasure

You say that you're not hiding it, but
   I know that you are.
   Your gray cloak is concealing it
   from those both near and far.
   And what is that great treasure that you
   hide beneath your wing
   as you vanquish all life's pleasantries and
   cease the birds to sing?
   Are you waiting to capitulate
   for yet another day?
   Or will you let the warmth return and
   chase it not away?
   I beg that you would acquiesce and
   Grant me this request.
   Unveil your golden secret
   In whose glory I might rest.

Rhythmic Lullaby

Steel on steel in waves of rhythm,
Rock-a-bye the babe to sleep.
Make sure grain gets where it's going.
See that horses get their feed.

Corn and barley, headed east.
Oats and sorghum, soybeans, wheat.
Crude and gravel, iron ore,
Building lumber, coal for power.

Headed where the people need,
Bound for where the cattle feast.
Stanza by stanza their schedules they keep,
Wheels gently humming a soft, soothing beat.

Steel on steel hauling wood, ores, and grain
While it lulls babes to sleep like a warm summer rain.
Stanza by stanza, the melody fades, and
The rhythm of steel becomes faint hues of gray.

Water from the Well

Refreshing to the soul it is, sweet water from the well.
   I love to go and draw it for to drink.
   As I am thus partaking of this cool and pleasant treat,
   I sit down for a while to stop and think.

   This treasure buried deep within the well is worth as gold.
   Consumed, it livens, quickens, quenches thirst.
   The stream, it knows not that my sip has been removed
   as it continues on its everlasting course.

   It satisfies but for a while, then I must go again
   to draw once more from this beloved well.
   And as I swallow each delightful, life-enriching gulp,
   my grateful soul begins to soar and swell.

   Carried off to heights unknown and places never seen
   to distant lands and peoples far and wide
   then brought back home and safely seated
   where I first began, the well and its sweet water at my side.

The Riddled Door

There is a door, a riddled door
   Beyond where most can see.
   Tangled vines obstruct its view,
   Along with brush and trees.

There is no knob upon the door,
Nor will you find a bell.
How and where one enters there
Only a few know well.

On the door, that riddled door,
Is but a single pane.
Very small, but yet it calls for
One to peer within.

Yet still the view is foggy, and
Demands a closer look,
As words and verse reveal more than
The cover of a book.

What lies beyond the riddled door
Is anybody's guess.
A wealth of knowledge? A kindred soul?
The bounty from a quest?

Rare the one who finds the key and
Unlocks riddled door, and
Rare the one who joyous reaps
The riches of its store.

I knew someone who dared to
Place his eye up to the pane.
In wonder, then, he sought the key
And finding it, went in.

I never learned what he had heard,
Nor what he may have seen, but
His face shone bright with great delight, and
He was never again the same.

A Riddle for My Son

In days of towers, castles, kings,
   And traveling minstrels who would sing,
   I came upon a man who held a box.

The man had traveled many days.
   Cloaked in secrecy, his ways,
   But never was he found without that box.

We sometimes saw him open it.
   We tried and tried to catch a glimpse
   Of what he had inside that little box.

We wondered, all, at what he had.
   What e'er it was made his heart glad.
   We thought there must be gold inside that box.

But feather-light it seemed to be.
Not heavy or obtrusive. What could be
Inside this ordinary box?

I've heard that all roads lead to Rome, but
I say all roads lead back home
Right to the very place they once began.

Yet here in Rome did this man stand
With box acquired in distant land.
Where was his home, and what was in his hand?

The riddle here is penned for you.
Veiled is the meaning. You have all the clues.
Read carefully, son. I have faith in you.

Dandelion

I'm a dandelion tucked
   within a bed of roses.
   Though tiny eyes delight in me,
   I'm not so loved by noses.

   Not like the pretty petals gracing
   tender stems and leaves;
   Not manicured or storied as
   the gifts they'll one day be.

   Yet thus endeared to all of those
   whose merry hearts still smile,
   A golden glimpse of sunshine are
   the flowers growing wild.

   Yes, a golden glimpse of sunshine are
   the flowers growing wild.

My Dream

Once upon a time, I wished
   for grand and splendid things:
   An acreage with sheep and goats,
   meadows fair, and springs,

   Tall and mighty oak trees
   reaching ever toward the sky,
   And all the lovely butterflies
   that nature could provide.

   I'd love a secret garden
   tucked away where none could see,
   A place of quiet solitude
   and creativity.

   Towering vines and luscious fruits
   and vegetables to eat,
   Surrounded by orange marigolds
   and zinnias soft and sweet.

Roses round the garden,
Rose of Sharon for the hedge,
And pretty little periwinkle
right at garden's edge.

I'd grow some grand tomatoes,
starting each new plant from seed.
Beside them I'd put peppers, parsley,
cucumbers, and peas.

Zucchini gets a special home
that produce may abound,
Planted three seeds at a time
in spacious garden mounds.

Garlic, onions, herbs, and roots,
I'd love to grow them all!
Strawberries and cauliflower,
and beans both short and tall.

Inside my home would be a hearth
with crackling fire's light,
A library with Christie, Noll,
and Scriptures to delight.

Volumes of poetry, hist'ry and prose
to cherish at end of day,
The Scriptures to teach me that
Jesus, the Christ, Is the one and only Way.

I know my little hobby farm
may never come to be.
I also know that if it won't,
that's still just fine with me.

I truly want a placid lea of sheep
beside a stream.
Yet 'tis always joy magnificent
to have it in my dreams.

Yes, if I find that my desires
on earth shan't come to be
I know that deep within my heart
it's still okay with me.

I truly want a placid lea of sheep
beside a stream, yet
'Tis always forward-thinking joy
to have it in a dream.

Word Waltz

Every time I take a look
  Inside the cover of a book,
  I'm always overjoyed at what I see.

For words and letters gracefully
Waltz off the pages, dance, and sing,
And paint a picture lovely as can be.

They tell me tales of long ago and
Lead me down less traveled roads.
I am always left still wanting more.

More captains, kings, and peasantry,
Knights, lords and ladies, chivalry,
More high-seas battles waged, more clanking swords.

More quiet walks in yonder woods,
More courage found, more trains that could,
More hope and faith beyond where eyes can see.

For words and letters gracefully
Waltz off the pages, dance, and sing.
They paint a picture lovely as can be.

Soft Falls the Rain

I close my eyes and drift away
To a land where whales and dolphins play.
A land where, at the end of day,
The sunset warms my heart.

My eyes still closed, I dream some more,
Now present on a different shore.
Crashing waves make my heart soar.
Their rhythm stirs my soul.

Not wanting yet the day to face,
I go to yet another place.
Its amber seas my spirit grace and
Still my restless mind.

Then one last vision do I see.
A field of lavender beckons me.
Aroma simple, pure, and sweet,
It grants me peace and joy.

Perhaps my eyes will thus remain
Gazing at oceans and fields of grain.
Or perhaps they will open and see through the pane
The beauty around me whilst soft falls the rain.

The Grand, Majestic Ball

Hidden in a little orb,
    yet still it grows and thrives
    In a dark and musty place,
    very much alive.

Reaching for its freedom and
a gleaming stroke of light,
Reaching through the suffocating dirt
with all its might.

It mustn't join its colleagues
'til the struggle here is through.
It cannot dance a stately waltz
until it's paid its dues.

It cannot don such striking dress
until it's grown quite tall.
Only then will it attend
the grand, majestic ball.

Every colleague thus appears
in exquisite attire.
Finest garments now they wear
whilst play the flute and lyre.

And in the gently blowing wind,
sweet sunshine on each face
They gift us with a lyric waltz
of elegance and grace.

Magnificent it is!
Stunning splendor, dazzling show.
Fleeting though the evening is,
how radiant the glow.

But then the clock strikes one last time and
they must go home, all,
Elated that they danced with poise at
the grand, majestic ball.

Take Me Somewhere

Take me somewhere beautiful.
   Take me some place grand.
   Take me on a new adventure
   Where I've never been.

   Show me brilliant painted sunsets.
   Show me starry nights.
   Show me a majestic sunrise,
   Deer at morning light.

   Mountains rising in the distance,
   Changing autumn leaves.
   Let me see a mighty eagle
   Floating on the breeze.

Dazzle me with sound and sight,
A strong and hearty brook.
Stun me with the Lord's creation
Everywhere I look.

Rivers wide and oceans deep –
I want to see them all!
Feel the warmth upon my face and
Hear the sparrow's call.

I'll never tire of the splendid
Wonders that I see.
I'll not grow weary of the days
I have you here with me.

SONG LYRICS

Still

Still.
Lord, help me to be silent while the
Voices around me just roar.
And Lord, help me to be quiet
And patiently trust what I've heard.

Lord, help me seek solitude
To pray and to read your Word.
I confess I need more of both
While I am here on this earth.
And I pray that you'll draw me
closer and closer to you.

For Lord, you are still,
Still my Redeemer and King.
You're still the reason I sing
And the theme of my song.

Still.
You are still on your throne up above
You still surround me with your love

Oh my God and my Lord.
Please help me to be still.

Grieve No More

You know you're not at home here
   Exiled in your own land
   Ruled by an enemy of the Lord,
   Subject to his demands.

You've waited for what seems like forever
For the Messiah to appear.
Oh, please dear Father in heaven,
Please hear our humble prayer.

In a lowly stable bare
Lay the babe, the infant King.
As the shepherds bowed before Him
The heavenly angels sang.

Child, open up your eyes.
See the glorious light above!
For God is in your presence now –
through His Son He sent His love!

Grieve no more. Wipe your tears away!
Unto you a Savior comes this day.
Grieve no more. Wipe your tears away!
Unto you a Savior comes this day.

You just laid Him to rest
In a cold and lonely grave.
You saw them crucify Him
Still you thought He'd save the day.

But you heard Him say "It's finished,"
As He gave up His last breath,
And the man you thought would save you
Has just succumbed to death.

Nothing pacifies your spirit
As you walk on toward the tomb.
Oh, the grief is overwhelming
And the fear of danger looms.

Child, open up your eyes.
See the sunlight up ahead!
He stands before you in victory.
He's defeated sin and death!

Grieve no more. Wipe your tears away.
For your Lord has risen on this day!
Grieve no more. Wipe your tears away.
For your Lord has risen on this day!

As you gaze into your mirror
At the sinner you know you are
The weight of guilt is heavy
You can't bear it on your own.

But the One who came for sinners
Has claimed you as His own.
Confess your sins to Jesus,
The King upon His throne.

He has conquered sin and death.
He has conquered your sin, too.
You've been made alive in Christ,
And you stand before Him new.

Child, open up your eyes.
Oh, behold your King!
Sing His faithfulness before Him.
Let His holy anthem ring.

Grieve no more. Wipe your tears away.
Your sins have been forgiven on this day!
Grieve no more. Wipe your tears away.
Your sins have been forgiven on this day!

Grieve no more. Wipe your tears away.
Behold the Lord is among us on this day!
Grieve no more. Wipe your tears away.
Our God reigns! Forever more He reigns.

Our God reigns! Forever more He reigns.
Our God reigns! Yes, forever more He reigns.

A Slave to Christ

Long ago I bore the mark of my captor.
  Beaten and abused, lonely and confused,
  Sin was my master.

  Chained to my wicked ways,
  dead in my sin to stay
    'Til your mighty hand reached deep down into the grave.

  Now I am dead to sin and alive to Christ, the Great King.
  He has rescued me. He broke the chains that held me.
  He paid the price to free me, and His glory now I see.
  I am a slave to Christ,
  And I've never, ever, ever been so free.

  Jesus, Master, Lion of Judah.
  You came for your name and
  Purchased me with your blood.
  You are King of every nation and
  Lord of all creation.
  We bow before you now and for all time.

  I am dead to sin and alive to Christ, the Great King.
  He has rescued me. He broke the chains that held me.
  He paid the price to free me, and His glory now I see.
  I am slave to Christ,
  But I've never, ever, ever felt so free.

I am free to praise the Father,
Free to praise the Son.
Free to praise the Spirit,
Godhead, Three in One. (twice)

I am dead to sin and alive to Christ, the Great King.
He has rescued me. He broke the chains that held me.
He paid the price to free me, and His glory now I see.
I am a slave to Christ,
And I've never, ever, ever been so free.

I am a slave to Christ,
And I've never, ever, ever been so free.

Old Man's Clothes

Why are you still wearing the old man's clothes
   Happy and content with the dark path you chose?
   You're stumbling around, brother, with both eyes closed,
   Pretending that you can see.

   You're floating face down in a cesspool of sin.
   Misery and death are your closest of friends.
   Isn't it time to let the Light shine in?
   Dear friend, you can repent and believe.
   For it's Jesus, the Savior, you need.

   You've been walking around in a church all your life.
   You even call yourself a believer.
   But Vanity Fair is your home and
   her goods are your jewels.
   Have you listened to the great deceiver?

   God the Father sent His Son, Jesus, the Christ
   To offer up His life as an atoning sacrifice.
   Then he rose from the dead and reigns forever on high.
   Brother, turn from your sin, and believe!

So why are you still wearing the old man's clothes
Happy and content with the dark path you chose?
Still stumbling around, brother, with both eyes closed,
Pretending that you can see.

You're floating face down in a cesspool of sin.
Misery and death are your closest of friends.
Open your eyes and let the light shine in!
Dear friend, you must repent and believe,
For it's Jesus, the Savior, you need!

The Potter

You call the weary and the heavy-laden
  To cast their every care upon you, Lord.
  Yet my stubborn spirit still defies you
  As if to say, "I can make it on my own."

What a foolish thought that is, that I am stronger
Than the one who made me out of the dust.
Oh, God, purge my selfish pride and let me rest in You.
By your grace, O Father, teach me how to trust.

You know me. You know my every thought.
Please cleanse my head, my hands, my heart, O God.
And please mold me into what you want.
You're the Potter; I am just the clay.
Please mend my heart and nourish my soul today.

Jesus paid the ransom for my sins.
His blood washed them all away.
There is no place I can run from His forgiveness.
I've no sin that His grace will not outweigh.

Lord, you took me out of darkness and into light.
You gave me peace and joy that know no end.
You turned my blindness into blessed sight.
I will praise your name again and again.

Oh, you know me. You know my every thought.
Please cleanse my head, my hands, my heart, O God.
And please mold me into what you want.
You're the Potter; I am just the clay.
Please mend my heart and nourish my soul today.

Empty-handed

Verse 1
What do I have to offer the King?
Not even the beat of my drum.
Broken, I wait alone in my room
Begging, "Lord, Jesus, please come."

CHORUS
Before His throne His praises should ring.
Impoverished, I have no offering to bring,
No merit to stand before a thrice-holy King.
So I come before the throne of God empty-handed.

Verse 2
If I had treasures and unmeasured wealth
Would I see the need for a King?
If I had my family, my friends, and my health
Would I still His praises sing?

CHORUS
Before His throne His praises should ring.
Impoverished, I have no offering to bring,
No merit to stand before a thrice-holy King.
So I come before the throne of God empty-handed.

BRIDGE
I have no breath in me. My heart's made of stone.
My eyes, they do not see His glory and His love.
I bring Him my darkness, all my sin and shame.
He gives me His righteousness, His glory, and His name.

CHORUS
Before His throne His praises should ring.
Impoverished, I have no offering to bring,
No merit to stand before a thrice-holy King.
So I come before the throne of God empty-handed.
Empty-handed.
Empty-handed.

Carry On

I don't need you just when the battle is over.
   I don't need you just when the fighting is done.
   I need you now in my darkest hour
   Locked arm in arm that I might have
   the strength to carry on.

   Friend, I thought I heard you say
   When my life settled down you'd come my way.
   Oh, but friend, can't you see I need you now
   When the battle is white hot and the chips are down.

   Can't you see I need you here with me?
   Together we'll secure a resounding victory.

   I don't need you just when the battle is over.
   I don't need you just when the fighting is done.
   I need you now in my darkest hour
   Locked arm in arm that I might have
   the strength to carry on.

Friend, I thought I heard you say
Everything will be fine. I'll be okay.
Oh, but friend, I know that you need me too
When troubles abound and friends are few.
I need you and friend you need me.
Together we'll secure a resounding victory.

I don't need you just when the battle is over.
I don't need you just when the fighting is done.
I need you now in my darkest hour
Locked arm in arm that I might have
the strength to carry on.

The strength to carry on.
Carry on. Carry on.
The strength to carry on.

Where Did the Time Go?

There's a newborn baby girl smiling up at me
   As I hold her safe and sound within my arms.
   It wasn't that long ago I held her mama so
   As she captivated me with all her charms.

   But a few more years have passed.
   Sand's run through the hourglass.
   And I cannot help asking once again.

   Where did the time go? Where did the years go?
   Can't get them back, I know.
   Curly little heads now tuck their own kids into bed.
   Where did the time go?

   It faded into memories that are stamped upon my heart.
   And they scattered like seeds upon the breeze
   Bringing us beautiful flowers.
   Where did the time go? Where did the years go?
   Can't get them back, I know.

There's a brand new baby boy due most any day.
I can't wait to sit and rock him on my knee.
It wasn't that long ago I held his daddy so
As I sang him songs my mama sang to me.

But a few more years have passed.
More sand through the hourglass.
And I cannot help asking once again.

Where did the time go? Where did the years go?
Can't get them back, I know.
Pretty little heads now tuck their own kids into bed, now.
Where did the time go now?

It was written like words on a page
And the chapter, it came to an end.
But as one chapter closes a new one can begin, can begin.

Little boys with curls fall in love with pretty little girls,
Oh tell me where did the time go now?
Pretty little girls grow up to wear lace and pearls,
Oh tell me where did the time go now?

Let the Children Come!

Let the little children come unto Me,
    For such is the kingdom of heaven.
    Don't turn them away,
    How I want them to stay
    For such is the kingdom of heaven.

    Let their little hearts beat free.
    Let their little feet follow after Me.
    Let the little children come unto Me,
    For such is the kingdom of heaven.
    Musical Interlude.

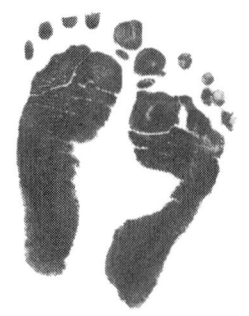

Let the little children come unto Me,
For such is the kingdom of heaven.
Don't turn them away,
How I want them to stay
For such is the kingdom of heaven.

Teach them to love my ways.
Teach them to follow Me all of their days.
Let the little children come unto Me,
For such is the kingdom of heaven.

Musical Interlude.

Let the little children come unto Me,
For such is the kingdom of heaven.
Don't turn them away,
How I want them to stay
For such is the kingdom of heaven.
Such is the kingdom of heaven.
Such is the kingdom of heaven.

King of My Heart

In the morning I will seek your face.
   In the afternoon I'll pray for your grace.
   In the evening I will thank you again
   For you are the King of my heart.

   Second Adam, perfect man.
   Holy God in flesh. The great I AM.
   Without blemish,
   Spotless Lamb of God.

   You sit Holy on your throne.
   You are worthy, God alone,
   To receive glory, honor, and power, and praise.

   Repeat from beginning, then continue below.

   In the morning I will seek your face.
   In the afternoon I'll beg for your grace.
   In the evening I will thank you again
   For you are the King of my heart.
   You are the King of my heart.
   You are the King of my heart.

Clean Hands and A Pure Heart

Clean hands and a pure heart,
   Lord, I ask of thee,
   For on my own, Lord,
   I could never know
   The riches of your mercy,
   And your never-ending grace,
   And your blood that washes
   My heart clean as snow.

In your tender kindness, Lord,
Oh how you loved me from the start.
Though I stood guilty, Lord,
Your forgiveness reached to me.
You breathed new life into
the lifeless creature I once was.
You drew my eyes and heart toward you, Lord,
And Your beauty now I see.

Lord, I give you thanks. Lord, I give you praise.
Lord, I give you honor and the glory due your name.
Lord, I give you thanks. Lord, I give you praise.
Lord, I give you honor and the glory due your name.
(Twice).

About the Author

Susan is a Christian author, poet, and songwriter. She began writing as a child, and she won her first two awards for her craft at the age of 10. She once had the privilege of meeting Wilson Rawls at a convention for young authors, and from that pivotal moment forward, her passion for writing has continued to grow.

Susan grew up in Missouri. At an early age, she fell in love with the rolling hills, caves, rivers, and rich landscape of the Ozark Mountains. The breathtaking views and the sounds of the countryside have captivated her, and she drew inspiration for much of her writing from them. No matter where she finds herself, she will always consider the Ozarks her home.

Susan is a member of the Society of Classical Poets (MSCP). In her spare time, she enjoys gardening, creating music, visiting beautiful places, and spending time with her family and friends.